HOW TO IMPROVE AT
SOCCER

*All the information you need to know
to get on top of your game!*

More than just instructional guides, the **HOW TO IMPROVE AT...**
series gives you everything you need to achieve your goals—tips on
technique, step-by-step demonstrations, nutritional advice, and the secrets
of successful pro athletes. Excellent visual instructions and expert advice
combine to act as your own personal trainer. These books aim to give you
the know-how and confidence to improve your performance.

Studies have shown that an active approach to life makes you feel happier
and less stressed. The easiest way to start is by taking up a new sport or
improving your skills in an existing one. You simply have to choose an
activity that enthuses you.

HOW TO IMPROVE AT SOCCER *does not promise instant success.*
It simply gives you the tools to become the best at whatever you
choose to do.

Every care has been taken to ensure that these instructions are safe to follow, but in the
event of injury Crabtree Publishing shall not be liable for any injuries or damages.

By Jim Drewett

 Crabtree Publishing Company
www.crabtreebooks.com

Cover: Soccer star Kaká (Ricardo Izecson dos Santos Leite)
Special thank you to: Chelsea Football Club, and
Elizabeth Wiggans
Photography: Roddy Paine Photographic Studios
Illustrations: Bill Bond

Photo credits: All Sport: p. 43 bottom; Action Images:
p. 44 center and bottom; Corbis: p. 45 bottom; Icon
SMI/Bob Van Der Cruijsevn/Pics United: front cover; ©
Shutterstock.com: Francisco Amaral Leitão: p. 45 top.

Library and Archives Canada Cataloguing in Publication

Drewett, Jim
   How to improve at soccer / Jim Drewett.

(How to improve at...)
Includes index.
ISBN 978-0-7787-3569-4 (bound).--ISBN 978-0-7787-3591-5 (pbk.)

1. Soccer--Training--Juvenile literature. I. Title. II. Series.

GV943.25.D74 2007   j796.334   C2007-904704-1

Library of Congress Cataloging-in-Publication Data

Drewett, Jim.
   How to improve at soccer / Jim Drewett.
      p. cm. -- (How to improve at--)
   Includes index.
   ISBN-13: 978-0-7787-3569-4 (rlb)
   ISBN-10: 0-7787-3569-9 (rlb)
   ISBN-13: 978-0-7787-3591-5 (pb)
   ISBN-10: 0-7787-3591-5 (pb)
   1. Soccer for children--Training--Juvenile literature. I. Title. II. Series.

GV944.2D74 2008
796.334083--dc22   2007030344

Crabtree Publishing Company
www.crabtreebooks.com   1-800-387-7650

Published in Canada
Crabtree Publishing
616 Welland Ave.
St. Catharines, Ontario
L2M 5V6

Published in the United States
Crabtree Publishing
PMB16A
350 Fifth Ave., Suite 3308
New York, NY 10118

Published by CRABTREE PUBLISHING COMPANY
Copyright © **2008**

CONTENTS

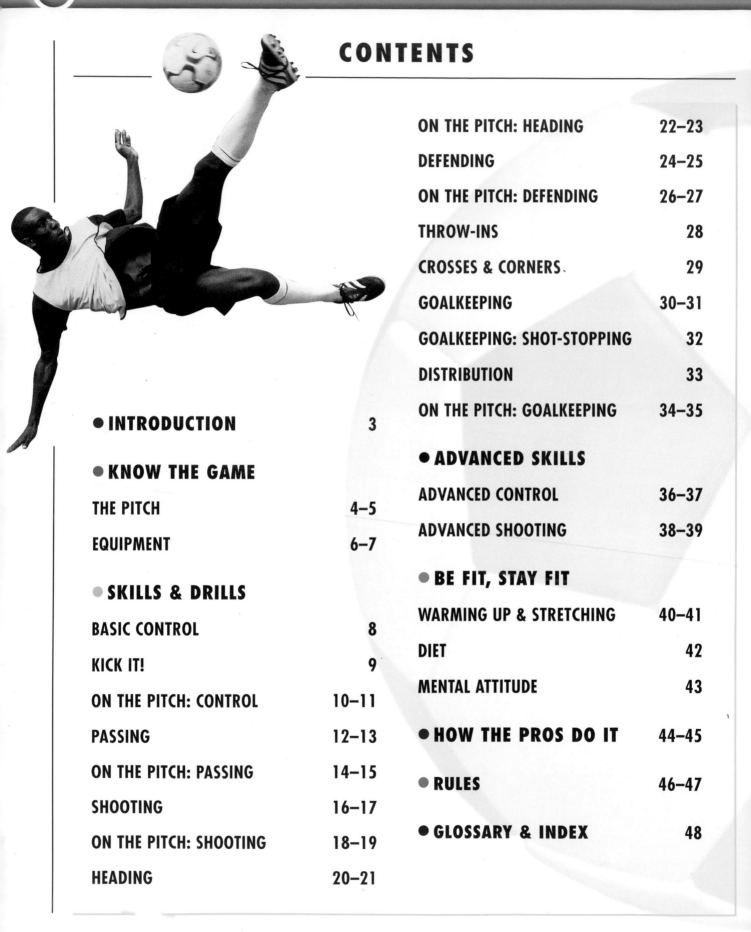

INTRODUCTION

It is called football in England, fussball in Germany, and voetball in Holland. In Spain it is known as futbol, while in Italy they get friends together for a game of calcio. Soccer is the most popular game in the world and is played in virtually every country on the planet.

GUIDE TO SYMBOLS & ARROWS

To help you understand movement and direction we have used the following:

The red color burst clearly demonstrates ball and body contact.

The orange coloring shows you the foot's point of contact with the ball.

The yellow arrow indicates the action of the body.

The red arrow indicates the direction of the ball.

The diagrams further clarify the action of the drill.

THE PITCH

*S*occer can be played almost anywhere, by any group of people. You can have a game in the park with four people, using only a ball and a couple of tin cans for a goal. Even a full-size game of soccer requires very little equipment.

THE PITCH

A soccer field, or pitch, can come in a range of sizes. According to the rules of FIFA (Federation of International Football Associations), a pitch must be between a maximum length of 130 yards (120 m) and a minimum of 100 yards (90 m), and a maximum width of 100 yards (90 m) and a minimum of 50 yards (45 m).

CORNER FLAGS

Corner flags must be a minimum of 5 feet (1.5 m) high for safety reasons and placed at each corner of the pitch.

GOALS

The crossbar on a full-size soccer goal is 8 yards (7.32 m) long and the posts are 8 feet (2.44 m) high.
The post and crossbar must be white in color so that they are easily seen. When sending the ball back into play, it must be kicked from inside the six-yard box.

TEAMS

A soccer match is made up of two teams of 11 players, each including 10 players and one goalkeeper. The teams can position their players in any formation they like. Teams can change players during the match with extra players called "substitutes". Most leagues allow three substitutes a match. The home team usually gets to choose the color of their uniforms.

SEVEN-A-SIDE

Many young players will begin playing competitive soccer in seven-a-side matches on a smaller pitch with smaller goals. This means that they will get more touches, or chances to play the ball. It is a great way to develop skills before playing eleven-a-side matches.

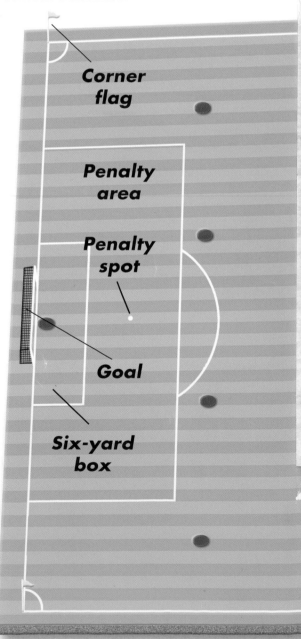

Corner flag

Penalty area

Penalty spot

Goal

Six-yard box

The referee is in charge of starting and finishing the match, and enforcing the rules of the game (see pages 46–47).

Previously known as linesmen, assistant referees help the referee make decisions. They use their flags to indicate throw-ins, corners, goal kicks, and offsides. The referee still has the final say on all decisions.

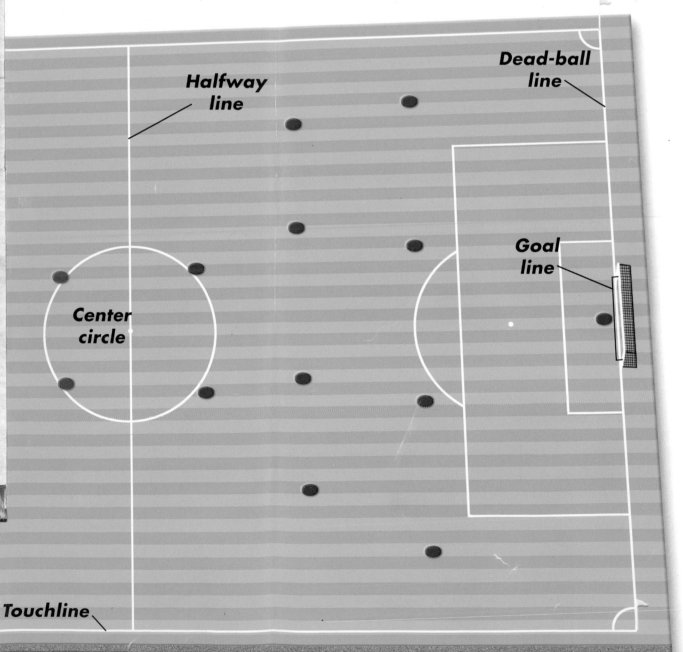

Halfway line

Dead-ball line

Goal line

Center circle

Touchline

EQUIPMENT

*I*t is important to feel comfortable when you are playing soccer. You can start with the proper uniform—now all you have to concentrate on is the game!

JERSEY

Soccer jerseys are made of light-weight material, so they don't slow your movement. Most also have tiny air-holes to keep the body cool.

SOCKS

Soccer socks are big enough to stretch over a pair of shinpads and tough enough to give some protection to the foot, ankle, and leg.

SHIN PADS

Players should always wear shin pads. Pads have hard plastic on the outside and a soft cushioning material inside. They are often held in place by an ankle guard and calf strap, and then covered by a sock.

SHOES

Shoes are the most important piece of equipment and must feel right. Most soccer shoes are called cleats and have short studs on the sole. Shoes are usually made of a combination of leather and plastic. They must be comfortable, but tough enough to protect the foot. Always pick a pair of shoes by how they fit, not what they look like. Choose the sole depending on the type of soccer that you will be playing— outdoor or indoor.

CLEATS: For use on soft and muddy grass pitches.

The stud (usually made of plastic with metal tips) come in varying lengths, pushing into the ground to give grip.

GOALKEEPING JERSEY

The goalkeeper's jersey needs to be stronger than that of an outfield player. Keepers slide across the ground far more often. The jersey is usually long-sleeved to give protection to the arms, and has built-in shoulder and elbow pads.

THE BALL

A full-size soccer ball is made from leather with a plastic coating to protect it. It has a circumference of 27–28 inches (67.5–70 cm) and must weigh between 16 ounces (450 g) and 14 ounces (410 g) at the start of the match.

GLOVES

Goalkeeping gloves are lightweight but extremely strong. The palm of the hand area is made from sticky foam-rubber, giving maximum grip. They are also designed to be much bigger than the hand that wears them. This design gives a wider surface area for catching the ball.

GOALKEEPING SHORTS

These shorts have padding around the hip area to help protect the keeper from falls.

BLADES: A modern alternative to studs. *Blades are longer and thinner than studs. The blades are designed to give excellent grip and comfort.*

TURF: For use on very dry grass, astroturf, and concrete pitches. *Turf boots have flat rubber soles designed to give grip on non-grass surfaces where studs won't work.*

MOLDED: For use on firm grass pitches and astroturf. *Molded cleats have rubber studs that are wider and shorter than normal studs are. They grip well on grass that isn't too soft or muddy, and can also be used on astroturf.*

BASIC CONTROL

Keeping possession and preventing the opposition from taking the ball is the name of the game. That is why you need to learn how to control the ball. If you have possession, it is much harder for your opponent to get it back, and much easier for you to pass it to a teammate or shoot for the goal.

TRAPPING THE BALL ON THE GROUND

As the ball comes toward you, open up your kicking foot at a right-angle to the other foot. As the ball meets the inside of your shoe, bring your foot back slightly to "cushion the ball".

Raise your foot just off the ground to meet the middle of the ball.

ON THE CHEST

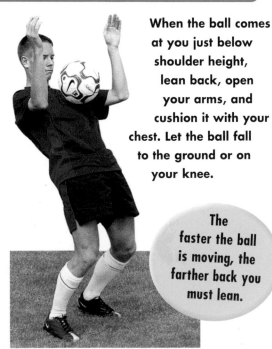

When the ball comes at you just below shoulder height, lean back, open your arms, and cushion it with your chest. Let the ball fall to the ground or on your knee.

The faster the ball is moving, the farther back you must lean.

IN THE AIR

When the ball bounces off the ground, get into position and raise your foot to meet it in the air. Cushion the ball with the inside of your shoe and let it drop gently to the ground.

ON THE KNEE

As the ball approaches at stomach height, let it come toward your body. Raise your thigh to form a platform to cushion the ball, then let it drop to your feet.

KICK IT!

Now that you've got the ball under control, use these four basic kicking skills to pass it on to a teammate.

THE SIDEFOOT

Bring your leg across slightly and use a short, sharp action to kick with the side of your foot. This punches the ball hard and fast along the ground.

STRAIGHT-ON VOLLEY

Draw back your kicking leg, and approach the ball head-on. Kick your leg straight out in front of you, meeting the ball with the front of your foot on the laces.

Always keep your eyes on the ball, your head still, and your body as steady as possible.

THE DRIVE

The drive hits the ball long and into the air. Approach the ball from behind, swinging your leg back to get more power. Contact is made at the bottom of the ball to scoop it up into the air while keeping it low.

THE SIDEFOOT VOLLEY

To accurately pass a ball in the air to a teammate, get into position as if to trap the ball in the air. This time, do not cushion the ball. Kick your foot up toward it to make contact and pass to your teammate.

ON THE PITCH: CONTROL

Here are three great drills to practice on the pitch to improve your ball control and balance. Try them either by yourself or with friends.

KEEPY UPPY (1 PLAYER OR MORE)

Playing keepy uppy on the field is a great way to improve your basic ball skills. Keep the ball off the ground, counting how many times you touch the ball before you lose control—then try to beat your record!

STEP 1
Try to play the ball with the front part of your foot, gently kicking the ball upward.

STEP 3
You can play the ball with both feet, your knees, chest, and even your head.

STEP 2
This will put backspin on the ball, keeping it close to your foot. Try to use both feet, not just your strongest one.

TRAPPING CIRCLE (2-6 PLAYERS)

Stand in a circle, with each player about 15 feet (3 m) apart. Then pass the ball to one another across the circle. Each player gets one touch to control the ball. Then they must quickly pass it on.

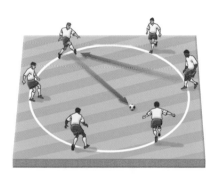

CONTROL & VOLLEY (2 PLAYERS)

This drill will help you control balls that come to you at an awkward height.

STEP 1

Two players stand a few yards apart. Player One then throws it gently to the other player, aiming anywhere between shoulder and knee height.

STEP 2

Player Two must control the ball with either the foot, knee, or chest, and then volley it back gently.

 TOP TIP
If you feel yourself losing balance, spread your arms out wide to help you regain control.

PASSING

Soccer is a team game. Once you have control of the ball, it is important for you to pass it on to your teammates. Passing keeps the ball away from your opponents.

SIDEFOOT PASSING

Using the inside of the foot is the most accurate way of passing the ball to a teammate. This pass is easier to receive, because it travels along the ground, not through the air.

STEP 1 *Step up to the ball with your non-kicking leg facing in the direction that you want the pass to go. Bring your kicking leg back.*

STEP 2 *Keep your eyes down and your head over the ball as you bring your kicking leg forward. Meet the center of the ball with the side of your foot.*

STEP 3 *Keep your head and body steady as you follow through. The power of the kick determines the distance that the ball travels.*

SIDEFOOT VOLLEYING

If the ball is off the ground and opponents are close to you, it is often best to pass with a sidefoot volley. This allows you to get the ball to a teammate quickly.

STEP 1 *Steady yourself and meet the middle of the ball with the side of your foot.*

STEP 2 *Keep your head down and your eyes on the ball. Aim for a teammate and follow through.*

LONG PASSING

To pass the ball over longer distances, you will need to use more power and get the ball in the air. Being accurate takes practice, but a perfect long pass to a teammate can take your opponent's defence by surprise and lead to goals!

STEP 1

Because you need more power, take a step or two back before kicking the ball. Spread your arms to give you balance and step forward as you swing your kicking leg right back.

STEP 2

Lean back slightly as you strike the bottom of the ball with the front of your foot.

STEP 3

Keep your head down, and follow through with your kicking leg.

TOP TIP

It is always easier to play the ball in the direction you are facing. Try to turn and face your teammate before passing.

ON THE PITCH: PASSING

*E*ven *if you have learned the basic skills of passing, it is important to keep practising.*
Pro players regularly use the drills featured here during training to sharpen their skills.

PASSING SQUARE (5 PLAYERS)

A great drill for improving passing and ball control.

Four players stand in a square with one (Player X) in the center. The ball is played to Player X, who traps it, turns 90 degrees to his right (or left) and passes it to the next player in the square. That player controls it and passes back to the center. Now Player X controls it, turns 90 degrees and plays it to the next player. Be sure that everyone gets a turn in the middle.

3-PLAYER PASSING DRILL

This drill enables you to play a long pass into the path of a teammate on the run.

Three players line up in a straight line, 16 feet (5 m) apart. Player B, in the center, plays the ball to Player A. As he does so, Player C sprints forward. Player A must control the ball, look up, and kick a long pass to Player C. The pass should be just in front of Player C.

LONG PASSING DRILL (2 PLAYERS)

This simple exercise will improve the accuracy of your long passing.

Two players stand opposite each other, starting at about 33 feet (10 m) apart. Play long passes to one another, lifting the ball in the air and aiming to place it at the feet. Move a little farther apart and keep passing.

PIGGY IN THE MIDDLE (4–10 PLAYERS)

Piggy In The Middle is perfect for getting you used to passing under pressure.

All of the players stand in a circle except for one who stands in the middle (Player X). The more players involved, the bigger the circle should be. The players around the circle must pass the ball to each other while Player X tries to intercept. If Player X touches the ball, the player who passed it must swap places and go in the middle. Start off allowing each player the chance to trap the ball before passing it. Later, use one-touch passing—players must pass the ball as soon as they get it.

 TOP TIP
If you have more than eight players in the circle, place two players in the middle.

SHOOTING

You can't win a soccer match without scoring goals, so shooting for goal is crucial. Much of the art of goal scoring is instinct, or reacting to a situation in an instant, but perfecting your shooting technique can increase your chances of success.

SIDEFOOT SHOOTING

Sidefoot shooting is for accuracy, when you're trying to line up a shot for the corner of the goal.

STEP 3
Bring your head and upper body forward as you make good, firm contact with the middle of the ball.

STEP 1
Keep the ball position in mind as you line up to shoot.

STEP 2
Make contact with the inside of your foot, angling your body toward the goal.

LONG-RANGE SHOOTING

To shoot from anywhere outside the penalty area, you will need a long-range shot. This shot has more power and height.

STEP 3
As always, keep your head down and your upper body forward as you follow through.

STEP 1
To gain power, you have to run to the ball, turning into the shot for added strength.

STEP 2
Stretch out your foot as you kick so that you make contact with the middle of the ball on the laces of your shoe.

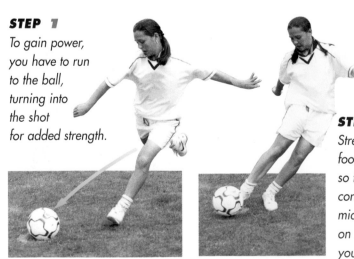

VOLLEYING

Volleying is a difficult skill to perfect. You must time your kick so that you connect cleanly with a moving ball. If you can learn how to volley well, it is a powerful shot.

Keep your balance with your arms and non-kicking leg as you follow through.

STEP 1
As the ball comes toward you in the air, spread your arms for balance, and get your body into position early.

STEP 2
Watch the speed and direction of the ball, twisting your body as you bring your kicking leg around to meet it.

Make contact with your shoelaces on the middle of the ball.

CHIPPING

Chipping is another clever skill to use if the keeper is off the goal line.

STEP 1
You do not need a big run or much power for a chip shot. Instead use a delicate touch to lift the ball.

STEP 2
Keep your head down and your body back. Approach the ball at an angle, and plant your non-kicking foot virtually right beside it.

STEP 3
Make contact with the bottom center of the ball. This gives the ball lift and scoops it up into the air. On contact, stop the kicking motion. This stabbing kick should put backspin on the ball, lifting it into the air.

TOP TIP
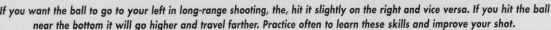
If you want the ball to go to your left in long-range shooting, the, hit it slightly on the right and vice versa. If you hit the ball near the bottom it will go higher and travel farther. Practice often to learn these skills and improve your shot.

ON THE PITCH: SHOOTING

*S*hooting is all about making the right decision on how and where to hit the ball. These drills are designed to help you get used to shooting quickly and hitting the ball on target every time.

TARGET PRACTICE (3–12 PLAYERS)

You've got a much better chance of scoring if you can hit the ball low and hard into the corner of the goal.

Place two cones or tin cans in a full-size goal guarded by a goalkeeper. The server, Player X, then stands on the edge of the penalty area. The other players stand outside the box and, one by one, pass the ball to the server. Player X one-touch passes it back into the box so the players can run to the ball and shoot. Aim for one of the gaps between the post and the cone.

 TOP TIP
Use the sidefoot shot in this exercise to give you the accuracy that you need to hit a small gap.

LAY-OFF SHOOTING (3–12 PLAYERS)

This drill is great for developing shooting skills around the edge of the box. It also trains players to react quickly to a lay-off, or quick sidefoot pass, from a teammate before striking.

STEP 1 ▶

The server, Player X, stands on the edge of the penalty area. The other players line up back toward the halfway line. One by one, they pass the ball to the server and run forward.

◀ STEP 2

The server lays the ball off into the player's path.

STEP 3

The player must adjust instantly to the lay-off and shoot first time at the goal, which is guarded by a goalkeeper.

VARIATION

Rather than laying the ball off, the server holds the ball and bounces it into the player's path. This means that the player must volley a bouncing ball toward the goal.

HEADING

Heading is an important skill to master, whether it be in defence or attack. You don't have to be tall to be a good header of the ball—the secret is timing and bravery.

BASIC HEADING

The basic principles of heading the ball are the same for attack and defence.

STEP 1

Watch the ball closely as it comes toward your head. Get your body into position so that you are right under the ball.

Aim to meet the ball on your forehead, keeping your eyes open and mouth shut. "Attack" the ball.

STEP 2

When the ball almost reaches you, tilt your head back slightly and then nod it forward to meet the ball. Tense your neck, arms, back, and leg muscles to make the contact strong.

JUMPING TO HEAD

Often, to win a header, you will have to meet the ball higher than head height. You must jump to meet it.

STEP 1

As the ball comes toward you, crouch down to give yourself spring. If the ball is really high you may have to run to gain power.

STEP 2

Time your jump so that you meet the ball at the highest point of your leap. Attack the ball with your forehead.

Backheading is particularly useful in attacking situations, adding a dangerous dimension to corners and throw-ins.

STEP 1

As the ball comes across, watch its flight, and position yourself so that you will be under the ball.

STEP 2

Rise to meet the ball. Try to meet the back of the ball with the top part of the back of your head.

STEP 3

As you make contact, throw your head back so that the touch is small. This motion makes the header difficult to defend.

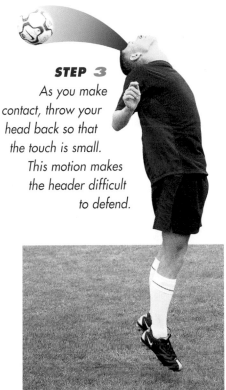

HEADING FOR GOAL

STEP 1

Get into position to meet the ball as early as possible so that you can be first to it. Lean back to be ready to nod the ball toward the goal.

When heading for the goal, try to direct your header downward. A low shot is much harder for a goalkeeper to save.

STEP 2

Get in a position so that your head is above the ball. Jump if you need to get higher. That way you can nod the ball down and into the goal.

ON THE PITCH: HEADING

These four simple heading drills are designed to improve your ability to deal with balls in the air. Just remember to focus on the ball at all times and be aggressive.

TWO-PLAYER DRILL

Two players stand 13 feet (5 m) apart. One player throws the ball into the air for the other to head back. The players should repeat this 20 times and then switch roles.

Don't worry too much about power in this drill. Just try to make good, solid contact with the ball.

CLEARANCE-HEADING DRILL (3 PLAYERS)

In defensive situations, you need to concentrate on getting distance on a clearing header. Try this drill to practice.

Three players stand in a straight line, 13 feet (5 m) apart. Player X (in the center) throws the ball into the air to Player A. Player A jumps to meet the ball and heads it back over Player X's head into the arms of Player B. Player X then repeats the drill. This time Player B heads the ball to Player A.

 TOP TIP
For clearance headers, power is more important than precise direction. Just get the ball out!

HEADING CIRCLE (PLAYERS 3–10)

Like all ball skills, heading can be used in many places on the pitch. A good way of ensuring that you are comfortable in all heading situations is to play "keep it up" in a heading circle.

Players stand in a circle 7-10 feet (2-3 m) apart and must keep the ball off the ground, using only their heads.

In a match, your opponents won't stand around and watch you head the ball—they'll be trying to win it too!

HEADING UNDER PRESSURE (3 PLAYERS)

This drill is the same as the two-player drill, but now a third player stands in front of the player who is heading the ball. This third player should not challenge for the ball. He should only make things difficult for his opponent.

When heading under pressure, take care not to foul your opponent. It is illegal to put your arms on his back or shoulders or push into him from behind.

DEFENDING

Defenders might not get the glory, but a last–ditch tackle or goal–line clearance is just as important to winning a match as a great goal is.

BLOCK TACKLE

Pulling off a successful block tackle requires strength, balance, and guts!

STEP 1
Get your body sideways to your opponent and wait for the right moment to pounce. When you see that your opponent has briefly lost control, make your move.

STEP 2
Go into the tackle leaning forward over the ball so that your body weight supports your leg. Make contact with the ball with the side of your foot.

Focus on the ball. You must be sure that you can win the ball if you're going for the tackle.

THE SLIDE TACKLE

The slide tackle is a move that requires split–second timing and great skill to pull off successfully.

STEP 2
Extend your kicking leg, and as you slide across your opponent's path, hook the ball away.

STEP 1
Watch the movement of the ball closely as you run beside your opponent. If you think that you can reach the ball, launch yourself across your opponent toward the ball.

A smart defender knows the right time to run in and steal the ball from under an opponent's nose.

STEP 1

Stick close to the shoulder of the attacker who you are marking and watch the play. When a chance to intercept a pass arrives, you are ready to pounce.

STEP 2

This ball is being passed to the attacker's feet. If he or she is slow to move or the pass is short, you can step in front of him or her and steal the ball.

Do not intercept if you don't think that you will get the ball. Stay in position.

Sometimes it is too risky for a defender to try to win the ball. If your opponent has it under control, the best tactic can be to jockey, or hold them up.

STEP 1

Position yourself in front of your opponent. Block the route to the goal with your body, forcing your opponent to go wide.

STEP 2

Continue to drop back, leaving the same gap between yourself and your opponent. Remain on your toes at all times. Be ready to switch sides or make a tackle if your opponent tries to get past you. Don't stand too close—a clever opponent will be able to push the ball around you easily.

ON THE PITCH: DEFENDING

The following drills are designed to recreate defensive situations so that defenders can practice their technique.

SLIDE CONE

It is not always a good idea to practice tackling each other, because players can get injured easily. Here is a non-contact slide–tackling drill with less risk of injuring you or your teammates.

STEPS 1, 2, 3
The player must run and slide tackle the ball without touching the cone.

JOCKEYING DRILL (2 PLAYERS)

This drill allows defenders to practice jockeying. Learn how to be patient and wait for the right time to make tackles.

Mark an area about 66 feet (20 m) long and 13 feet (5 m) wide. Use cones to mark out three gaps of 10 feet (3 m) across, as shown in the diagram on the next page. An attacking player is given the ball at one end of the area. This player must pass through the center of all of the cones to the end of the area. A defending player jockeys him all the way, but must not tackle at any point. The defender tries to force the attacker to play outside the cones.

INTERCEPTION DRILL (3 PLAYERS)

By making drills like this competitive, you can make practice more exciting.

Mark out an area of 23 x 23 feet (7 x 7 m). An attacking player and a defensive player stand within this area, with the defensive player marking the attacker and the attacker trying to lose the marker. Another player stands on the edge of this area and tries to pass to the attacker's feet. The defensive player tries to intercept the ball. The attacking player wins a point by collecting a pass. The defending player wins a point by getting a touch and making the interception. The first player to 10 points wins.

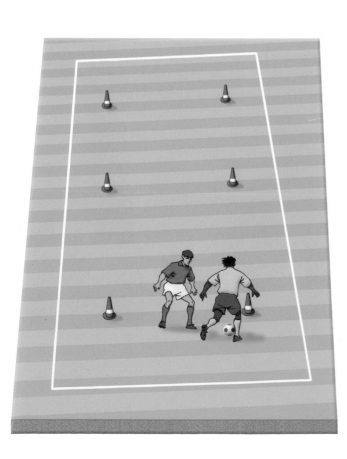

THROW-INS

I t is important to keep possession for your team at a throw-in, which means that the delivery must be right.

SHORT THROW

With all throws, the ball must be held in both hands. It must go fully back behind the thrower's head and be released in one smooth movement above the head. Both feet stay on the ground behind the touchline.

STEP 1
Stand up straight with the palms of both hands spread across the back of the ball. Take it behind your head.

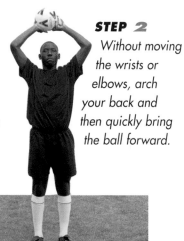

STEP 2
Without moving the wrists or elbows, arch your back and then quickly bring the ball forward.

STEP 3
Release the ball when it is directly over your head, and follow through with your hands.

LONG THROW

To get more distance and power on a throw-in, take a short run to the line and put your back into it.

STEP 1
Take a couple of steps back from the line. Grasp the ball firmly with both palms across the back of it.

STEP 2
Begin to step forward. As you do, bring the ball back behind you and run up to the line.

STEP 3
Plant your leading leg firmly into the ground and, as you take the ball behind your head, arch your back.

STEP 4
In a steady and powerful motion, use your shoulders and arms to propel the ball forward over your head.

CROSSES & CORNERS

People love players with great finishing, or goal–scoring, skills. But sometimes the greatest skill is in making the perfect pass that creates the chance to score.

STEP 1 Approach the ball from an angle. If you are right-footed, approach it from the right and vice versa.

STEP 2 Spread your arms for balance and plant your non-kicking leg behind the ball.

CROSSING

During a match, it is rare to get into a good position to cross the ball. When it happens, try to place the ball in a dangerous spot.

STEP 3 Aim to make contact with the side of the ball, and follow through. This way, your kick should curve the ball away from the keeper and toward an open teammate.

STEP 1 A right-footed player takes it from the left, while a left-footed player takes it from the right.

STEP 2 The kick curves the ball in toward the goal.

TAKING INSWINGING CORNERS

By swinging the ball into the goal, you put the goalkeeper and defenders under immense pressure at their own goal.

STEP 1 An outswinging corner incorporates all of the above crossing skills.

STEP 2 A left-footed player should take a left-hand corner, and a right-footed player should take one from the right.

TAKING OUTSWINGING CORNERS

Swinging the ball away from the goal makes it risky for the goalkeeper to come out to catch it. The keeper doesn't want to be too far out of the goal, so the ball is left for an attacking player.

GOALKEEPING

O*ne glorious save can make the goalkeeper a hero, but most of time, goalkeeping is about good positioning and ball handling. If a keeper has these skills, a spectacular save may not be needed. Remember, the simple stops or catches are just as important as the incredible ones are. Both of them keep the ball out of the net!*

GATHERING THE BALL

Shots into the chest should be gathered into the stomach. If you stand up straight, the ball could easily bounce back out.

STEP 1
Allow your body to absorb the shot by bending over and gathering the ball in.

STEP 2
Once the ball has come into your stomach, wrap your hands around it so it cannot escape.

BASIC CATCHING

When catching a ball at head height, you must get your hands behind the ball, no matter how simple the catch may appear. Sometimes, these simple catches can slip through an over-confident goalkeeper's hands. Never think that a catch is made until the ball is safely in your hands.

LOW STOP

There is nothing worse for a goalkeeper than letting a shot slip through his legs, so make sure that it doesn't happen.

Go down on one knee. This knee blocks the ball in case it slips through your hands. Your legs should form a "K" shape. Use your hands to gather the ball into your body.

STEP 1 *Take a two or three step run-up to launch yourself into a higher jump.*

STEP 2 *As you leap into the air, begin to lift your arms as you watch the movement of the ball.*

HIGH CATCHING

It is important to catch crosses and high balls into the box at the highest point possible.

STEP 3 *Catch the ball and hold on tight. Gather the ball into your body as you fall so it's not knocked loose.*

PUNCHING

If the penalty area is crowded with players, you may not be able to get a clear chance to catch the ball. In this case, punch the ball away.

ONE-HANDED

One-handed punches are required when you need to reach over a crowd of players to clear a ball. Clench your fist and extend your arm to its farthest reach to punch the ball clear.

TWO-HANDED

The secret of a good punch is to make solid contact so that the ball travels far. Using two hands gives you a greater chance of making good contact. Clench your fists, hold them together and punch the ball at the highest point that you can reach it.

GOALKEEPING: SHOT-STOPPING

Good goalkeeping is about getting the simple things right, such as catches and saves. But a goalkeeper needs a little extra skill and practice to pull off fingertip or diving saves.

DIVING SAVE

Shot-stopping requires good eyes and quick motions. It is important to hold on to the ball after making a save. If that's not possible, push the ball out of play or away from danger.

STEP 1 *As the shot comes in, shift your body weight to the side that the ball is approaching. Get your hands ready to stop it early.*

STEP 2 *Spread your hands so that your lower hand will stop the ball and your upper hand will come down on top of it to prevent it from bouncing away.*

STEP 3 *Bring your body down behind the ball as an extra line of defence. Bring the ball into your chest as you drop down on top of it.*

DISTRIBUTION

Agoalkeeper who has good distribution skills can add a whole new dimension to his or her team. A well-directed kick or throw can instantly turn your team from defence to attack.

HIGH THROW

Good for accurate longer balls.

STEP 1 *Lean back and twist your arm so that the ball is held above instead of below your wrist. Keep your arm straight as you bring your upper body forward and aim.*

STEP 2 *The farther you need to throw it, the earlier you release the ball. Follow through to get maximum power and direction.*

LOW THROW

For accurate short balls to a player's feet.

Swing your arm forward and go down onto one knee so that the ball rolls smoothly along the ground. This pass makes it easier for the player receiving the ball to control it.

PUNT

Less accurate but very long distance.

STEP 1 Hold the ball, cupped in both hands, ahead of you, and concentrate on it. Take a two or three step run-up and release the ball, swinging your kicking leg back as you do so.

STEP 2 Focus on the ball as you kick it. Aim your kick under the ball to lift it into the air and across the pitch.

ON THE PITCH: GOALKEEPING

Goalkeepers sometimes spend a lot of the match with little or nothing to do. It is important for them to practice their handling skills and sharpen their reflexes. These four pro drills will help make sure that they are always ready for the ball.

BALL AT KEEPER (2 PLAYERS)

This drill is great to use in training to test a goalkeeper's handling, and it can also be used before a game as a warm-up exercise.

A player stands on the six-yard line with the ball in his or her hands. He or she then drops it and half-volleys it at the goalkeeper. The keeper must catch it cleanly, gather it in and then return it each time. The server varies the height and power of the shot each time.

ON THE DECK (2 PLAYERS)

This drill is designed to work on a goalkeeper's handling skills. It also helps build up agility and upper-body strength.

STEP 1 *The goalkeeper lies on his or her back with his or her shoulders forward and his or her hands set while a player throws the ball to him or her.*

STEP 2 *With the ball aimed to his or her left, right, or directly at him or her, the goalkeeper stretches backward or to one side to make the catch.*

STEP 3 *The goalkeeper rocks forward and returns the ball to the server in one movement, ready for the next throw.*

CATCHING DRILL (3 PLAYERS)

Goalkeepers must be able to catch a high ball in a crowded penalty area. This drill is designed to recreate the pressure of a real match for a goalkeeper.

One player, the server, stands at one corner of the six-yard box. An attacking player stands in front of the goalkeeper at the far post, two yards off of the goal line. The server throws the ball into the air above the attacker for the goalkeeper to catch.

PUNCHING VARIATION

Goalkeepers can use this same drill to practice their punching. Try using one or two more players in the six-yard area to obstruct the keeper.

 TOP TIP
If a low cross is hit to the front post or the center of the goal, move towards the ball, and get in front of attacking players. You must reach the ball before them.

ADVANCED CONTROL

Once you have mastered the basics of soccer, you can become more adventurous. Instead of looking for the easy pass, test your skills to the maximum.

DRIBBLING

Running quickly with the ball under control can help you unlock the tightest defences.

STEP 1 The secret of good dribbling is to keep the ball close to your feet at all times. As you run with the ball, drop your shoulder and swerve your upper body. These motions make it more difficult for defenders to decide where you're going.

STEP 2 Move the ball from one foot to the other, keeping it as close to you as possible. If you can, use sudden body movements and foot skills to confuse and get past your opponents.

THE BACKHEEL

The backheel is not a difficult skill to master, but you must be careful. Always stay aware of the space around you and the movement of your teammates behind you before passing.

STEP 1 As you move with the ball and know a teammate is moving behind you, simply move your kicking leg over the ball.

STEP 2 Kick backwards with your heel, making good, firm contact with the middle of the ball.

CRUYFF TURN

The Cruyff turn—named after the great Dutch player of the seventies, Johan Cruyff—is a good way of finding space when you are closely marked. The trick uses surprise to buy you some time.

STEP 1 Moving forward with the ball, stretch out your arms and lift your kicking foot as if you are about to kick the ball.

STEP 2 Instead, step over the ball with your kicking leg.

STEP 3 Twist your body back in the other direction. At the same time, flick the ball back with the inside of your foot.

STEP 4 Complete the 180 degree turn and move away with the ball.

THE STEP-OVER

The step-over is a great trick to use to get past a player.

STEP 1 As you meet a defender, move your kicking foot inside the ball as if you're about to flick it around him or her with the outside of your shoe.

STEP 2 Instead of flicking the ball with your kicking foot, step over it. This move can confuse your opponent.

STEP 3 Shift your body weight the other way, and flick the ball with your other foot to get around the defender.

STEP 4 Run past the defender on the other side. Often, the defender is caught off balance by this trick.

ADVANCED SHOOTING

It is rare to get an easy shooting chance in soccer. Sometimes you have to do something quite special to score a goal—like one of these shots!

OVERHEAD KICK

This is the one of the hardest soccer skills to execute, but when done well, it can be spectacular.

STEP 1 You can only try an overhead kick if the ball is coming across you in the air when you have your back to the goal. If you think that you can perform an overhead kick, watch the flight of the ball, begin to lean back, and shift your weight onto your kicking leg.

WARNING: The overhead kick is extremely athletic, so be very careful when practicing it. Make sure that you land on soft grass, sand, or a mat.

STEP 2 Focus on the flight of the ball as you stretch your arms out. Continue to lean back, and bring your non-kicking leg up.

STEP 4 At the last moment, spring off with your kicking leg, crossing your legs like scissors in midair for balance. Make contact with the ball as your body is parallel to the ground. Extend your foot toward your head so that you kick the ball over your shoulder.

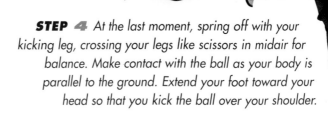

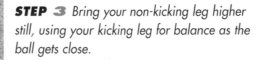

STEP 3 Bring your non-kicking leg higher still, using your kicking leg for balance as the ball gets close.

CURLING THE BALL

Curling the ball is another difficult skill. The secret is to kick through one side of the ball. This motion puts a spin on it as you follow through.

STEP 1 *Approach the ball from an angle of about 90 degrees. If you are right-footed, the goal should be to your left and vice versa.*

STEP 2 *Run up to the ball and strike it, aiming for the side. Make contact with the inside of your foot, and twist your body toward the goal. These motions help create the spin that curls the ball.*

OUTSIDE OF THE FOOT

STEP 1 *Approach the ball from the opposite side than the inside curled shot shown above. For example, right-footed players now have the goal to their right. Approach at about a 40 degree angle. Strike the near side of the ball with the outside of your shoe.*

STEP 2 *Follow through in the same way as before, keeping your body forward and your head down.*

TOP TIP
For curled shots that require height and distance, hit the ball on the side but toward the bottom. For shots that travel just off the ground, strike the ball on the side but more toward the top to keep the ball down.

WARMING UP & STRETCHING

Warming up and stretching before a practice or a match is very important. It reduces the chances of injury and increases a player's speed and ability to twist and turn.

WARMING UP

Before you kick a ball or even begin stretching, you must first warm up your body. This reduces your chance of pulling a muscle or a tendon (the cause of more than half of all soccer injuries). All you need to do is a light jog for five minutes. This will increase your heart rate and get the blood pumping around your body.

STRETCHING

You must be very careful with your stretching.

- *Never stretch until the body is warmed up.*
- *Always stretch slowly and gently and never so much that it is uncomfortable.*
- *Hold each stretch for 10 to 20 seconds, keeping your body steady at all times.*
- *Never rock or bounce on a stretch.*
- *Breathe out as you stretch.*
- *Stretch both before and after exercise.*

There are many stretches, but here are some of the most important ones. Ask a coach or a physiotherapist to show you others, and check that you are doing them correctly.

HAMSTRING STRETCH

Kneel on the ground and stretch one leg out in front of you. Put your heel in the ground and point your toe in the air until you feel slight tension in the hamstring (this runs down the back of the thigh). Once the tension dies down, pull your toes toward you for a further stretch.

PELICAN THIGH STRETCH

Stand on one leg, holding the foot of your other leg behind your buttocks with your knees close together. Keep your balance and stretch.

GROIN STRETCH

Sit on the ground with the soles of your feet together and your knees bent, pointing away from you. Then use your elbows to press your knees down. You will feel a gentle stretch in the groin area.

TWO'S COMPANY

Some stretches can be done with a teammate. This develops better balance. Keep the stretch steady and safe.

CALF STRETCH

Put the weight of your body on the front foot. Bend at the knee, and stretch the other leg behind you with the weight resting on your toes. Then lean forward so that your hands touch the ground, and slowly push your outstretched leg back.

DIET

Eating certain foods won't improve your soccer skills, but you can give yourself more energy and stamina on the pitch by eating and drinking a balanced diet. This food chart gives you the basic principles of a balanced diet, ideal for all athletes.

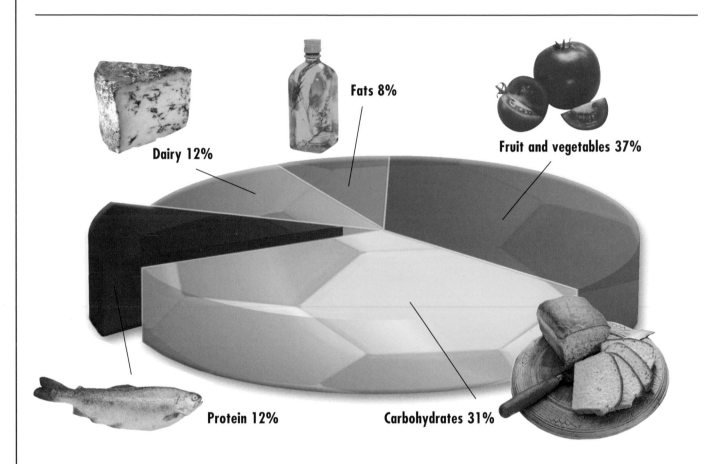

Dairy 12%

Fats 8%

Fruit and vegetables 37%

Protein 12%

Carbohydrates 31%

ENERGY BUSTERS

If you are doing a lot of exercise, cut down on fatty foods and eat plenty of carbohydrates. These foods provide more energy for the exercise that you are doing.

Protein is required for the growth and repair of the body, but try to choose low-fat sources.

BEFORE THE MATCH

To produce the maximum energy before a match or training, you should eat a high-carbohydrate meal at least three hours before the game.

Low-fat pasta or rice dishes (with no creamy sauce) are ideal. Around a half hour before the game, boost your carbohydrate levels with fast-digesting snacks, such as bananas or dried fruit. It is crucial to drink plenty of liquid before a game. Drink water or isotonic sports drinks two or three hours before playing to make up for the water that you'll sweat away when playing.

MENTAL ATTITUDE

It is important to prepare the mind as well as the body for a soccer match or even a practice. When you are confident, relaxed and believe in yourself, your playing will improve. If you believe that you will score the penalty, then the chances are that you will.

MIND & BODY

The strength of a soccer player comes from both mind and body.
It is important to do many forms of exercise to strengthen all areas of your body. Strong concentration and quick thinking are needed on the pitch. Full physical fitness makes the mind more alert and decisive.

MENTAL PREPARATION

Before a match, focus your mind on the game ahead. Visualize certain match situations and think about how you would deal with them in your head.
Picture yourself scoring the goal, making the spectacular save, or the last moment tackle. Focus your mind on the game as an individual player and as a team. Your team captain or coach can help you do this. Staying positive will help you have fun and play hard. If you believe that you can win, you will have a better chance.

HOW THE PROS DO IT

Imagine playing soccer every day AND getting paid for it! It sounds great, but don't think that it is all fame and glory. It takes hard work and dedication to make it to the top and stay there. The modern soccer player maintains high levels of performance by sticking to a strict diet and getting plenty of sleep.

TYPICAL TRAINING DAY

7.30	Wake up
8.00	Eat low-fat, high-carbohydrate breakfast
9.15	Arrive at training ground
9.30	Change into uniform
10.00	Warm up and stretching
10.30	Training

- Fitness work: sprints, circuits, and jogging
- Ballwork: control and passing drills
- Specific coaching: defence, midfield, and attack
- 11-a-side practice match
- Shooting and set-piece practice

1.30	Shower and change
2.00	Lunch
3.00	Team meeting: discuss tactics for the next match
4.00	Home

TYPICAL MATCH DAY

9.00	Wake up
9.30	Light breakfast of cereal and fruit
11.00	Leave for ground
12.00	Pre-match meal: chicken and pasta
1.00	Team meeting
2.00	Get changed
2.15	Warm up
2.45	Team talk
2.55	Leave dressing room for pitch
3.00	Kick off
3.45	Half time
4.00	Second half
4.45	Final whistle
5.00	Post-match interviews
5.30	Cool down, then soft drinks in the Players' Lounge
6.30	Return home

TRAVELING TO MATCHES

Not all matches are home games, and modern soccer players spend a huge amount of time traveling to away and international matches.

If the away match is more than 100 miles (160 km) away, teams usually travel the day before the game and stay in a hotel near their opponents' stadium. Then on the day of the match, they can rest and focus on the game ahead. For international matches, teams will fly out a day or two before the match. Players picked to play for their countries may have to fly to the other side of the world for a game!

MONEY

Soccer players in Britain's Premiership, Italy's Series A or Spain's La Liga earn huge amounts of money, but most professional soccer players do not.

The world's best players receive large sponsorship deals and other benefits, but all of them would say that they play because they love the game of soccer, not just money.

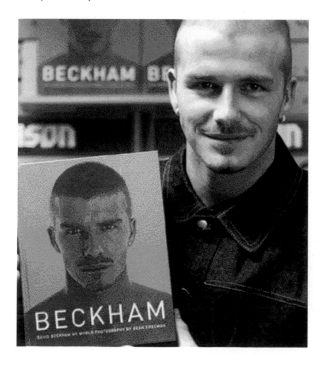

MEDIA WORK

If you are a top player, everyone wants to know your opinion.

There are hundreds of TV and radio shows, newspapers, magazines, and web sites dedicated to soccer. Part of the soccer player's job is to do interviews and pose for photos. Some players enjoy this, while others hate it. Even small league players can't avoid reporters for too long. Talking with the media helps fans learn about their team.

RULES

As with all sports, rules are designed to ensure that play is fair and safe. These are the basics, and they are always enforced by the referee.

THE OBJECT

To score more goals than the other team. The winning team is the one that scores the most goals. If both sides score none, or the same number, the result is a draw. Whether a match goes to extra time, golden goal, or penalty shoot-outs depends on the rules of the competition in which the game is being played.

TIME

A standard eleven-a-side football match lasts 90 minutes, with two halves of 45 minutes, plus injury time at the end of each half. The length of injury time is decided by the referee.

THE BALL

The ball can be played by any part of the body other than the arm OR hand. Dangerous kicking, going for the ball when it is in the air and near another player's head, is not allowed. If a player is guilty of handling the ball or dangerous kicking, a free kick is awarded to the opposition.

A GOAL

A goal is scored when the ball goes between the posts and under the crossbar of the goal structure. It must completely cross the goal line either along the ground or in the air. When a goal is scored, play is restarted with a kickoff by the team that was just scored upon.

FREE KICKS

A free kick is awarded by the referee when a foul is committed or a player is offside. A kick is awarded to the team on which the offence was committed. All opposition players must be at least 10 yards (9 m) from the ball when the kick is taken.

Most free kicks are direct and can be used to score. Certain offences, such as obstruction, cause an indirect kick. This kick means that the attacking team cannot score directly from it. The ball must touch at least one other player, on either team, before a goal can be scored.

PENALTIES

A penalty kick is awarded when a player from the defending team commits a foul against an attacking player inside the penalty area. The attacking team must nominate one player to take the kick from the penalty spot. The rest of the players on the pitch stand outside the penalty area and the "D". If he or she scores, then a goal is awarded.

The goalkeeper may move sideways along the line before the kick, but he or she cannot move forward until after the kick is taken. If he or she does so, the kick must be taken again. The penalty taker is not allowed to touch the ball again until another player, from either team has done so.

OFFSIDE

At the exact moment that the ball is played forward by an attacking player, there must be at least two defending players (including the goalkeeper) between or level with the farthest forward attacking player and the goal. This rule does not apply if the farthest forward attacking player is within his own half.

BACKPASS LAW

A goalkeeper is not allowed to touch the ball with his hands if it is intentionally passed to him by a teammate. If he does so, an indirect free kick is awarded.

SIX-SECOND LAW

After a goalkeeper has picked up the ball, he must release it within six seconds. However, during that time, he can take as many steps as he wants.

YELLOW CARD

Known as a caution, this is issued to a player who has committed a particularly bad foul or who has repeatedly offended. There are also certain offences that merit an automatic yellow card, such as deliberate handball and kicking the ball away after the whistle has blown.

RED CARD

If a player is issued a red card by the referee, he or she must leave the field of play immediately. Certain offences require an automatic red card, such as fighting or handling the ball on the goal line to prevent a goal. If a player is awarded two yellow cards within the same match, he or she is automatically issued a red card.

GOAL LINE

If the ball completely crosses this line legally, then it is a goal.

DEADBALL LINE

If an attacking player sends the ball completely across this line, a goal kick is awarded. If a defending player does this, then a corner kick is awarded.

TOUCHLINE

If the ball completely crosses this line, possession of the ball is given to the opposing team for a throw-in.

PENALTY AREA

This is the only area on the pitch where the goalkeeper is allowed to touch the ball with his hands. When a defending player commits a foul inside the area, a penalty kick is awarded to the opposition, unless the offence is an indirect free-kick offence, such as obstruction, or the goalkeeper handles a backpass. In this case, an indirect free kick is awarded.

THE "D"

When a penalty is awarded, all players (apart from the goalkeeper and the kicker) must be outside the penalty area, and outside this small "D".

SIX-YARD BOX

Goal kicks can be taken from anywhere within the six-yard box.

PENALTY SPOT

Where penalty kicks are taken from. On a full-size pitch it should be 12 yards (11 m) from the center of the goal.

HALFWAY LINE

This marks the halfway point in the length of the pitch.

CENTER CIRCLE

A circle 10 yards (9 m) across in the center of the pitch. Opposition players must be outside the center circle on their side of the pitch when the other team is taking a kickoff.

GLOSSARY

ATTACKER – A player whose main objective is to score goals and create scoring chances for others.

BACKPASS – A ball played backwards to a player or to his or her own goalkeeper.

CHIP – A lofted pass or shot.

CORNER KICK – A ball kicked from the point where the touchline meets the deadball line. Given after a defending player has played the ball over the deadball line.

DEFENDER – A player who generally plays close to his or her own team's goal whose main objective is to prevent the opposition from scoring.

FOUL – Any piece of play or incident on the pitch that breaks the rules and regulations of the game.

GOAL – A point-scoring play when the ball legally crosses the goal line, under the crossbar and between the posts. The word is also used for the structure created by posts, a crossbar, and a net.

GOALKEEPER – Responsible for preventing the opposition's ball from entering the net and scoring a goal. The only player on the pitch who is allowed to use his or her hands to play the ball. He or she can move anywhere on the pitch but cannot handle the ball outside his or her team's penalty area.

HEADER – Legal playing of the ball with the head, usually the forehead.

LAY OFF – Short pass into the path of a teammate.

MIDFIELDER – A player who generally plays in the space between his or her team's attack and defence, combining the roles of attacker and defender.

PASS – An intentional ball played to a teammate.

SAVE – A play made when a goalkeeper successfully intercepts a strike on goal.

SHOT – An attempt at goal.

THROW IN – A two-armed overhead throw from the touchline, used after the ball has gone out of play.

VOLLEY – A kick where the foot meets the ball in the air before it touches the ground.

WALL – A voluntary line-up of defenders to protect their goal at a free kick. Must be at least 10 yards (9 m) from the ball.

INDEX

Printed in the USA